To my Mom for being patient with this very impatient beginner

and to my first students who inspired every lesson in this book

Happy Sewing!
XO, Angeline

The Impatient Beginner's Guide to Sewing

2nd Edition

by

Angelina McCullar

BlueprintDIY

formatted & edited by

Kachelle Parker

LET'S GET STARTED!

Table of Contents

Introduction

- Why This Book is Different

1. Parts of the Machine and Sewing Tools 1
- What you need to get started 2
- Where to buy 5
- More sewing tools 5
- What kind of sewing machine do I need? 7
- Parts of a sewing machine 10

2. How to Set Up Your Sewing Machine 15
- How to wind the bobbin 17
- How to thread a sewing machine 17
- How to load the bobbin 18
- Types of needles 19
- Types of threads 21

3. Practicing - How to Sew 23
- Practice These Skills 24
- How to Cut & Pin 26

4. How to Care for your Sewing Machine 27
- Sewing Machine Care 28
- Common Sewing Machine Problems 30

5. What If I Mess Up? 37
- Tips to Keep You Going 38

- How to Seam Rip 40

6. Learn How to Measure Yourself 43

7. How to Read a Pattern 49

- Understanding the Pattern Envelope 50
- Pattern Pieces 52
- Instruction Sheet 53
- Cutting Your Fabric 54
- Where to Find Patterns 55

8. Types of Fabric 59

- Fabric Guide 60
- Tips for Choosing the Right Fabric 62
- How to Work with Different Textiles........... 64

9. Finishing Seams 67

10. First Project Recommendations 73

- Pillow Case 74
- Skirt with elastic band 75
- Ruffle Tote Bag 78

8. Final Words of Encouragement 81

- Next Steps 82

Glossary 84

Notes 92

Practice Sheets 96

Introduction

Welcome to "The Impatient Beginner's Guide to Sewing." This book is designed for those who are eager to dive into the world of sewing with a sewing machine but want to skip the lengthy tutorials and **get straight to the basics**. Whether you've just bought your first sewing machine or you're curious about picking up a new hobby, this guide will walk you through the essentials with concise, easy-to-follow chapters. We've included QR links to videos that demonstrate each step, so you can see exactly how things are done. Let's start this creative journey together and transform fabric into fantastic projects with confidence and ease.

Why This Book is Different
Most sewing books throw a mountain of information at you, which can be a bit overwhelming, right? Not Here! We're cutting out the fluff and focusing on quick, easy tips and shortcuts. You'll get **all the good stuff without the headache**.

How to Navigate This Guide
The important things are bold, so if you're not a reader look for the bold text and watch the tutorials. To watch tutorials, **scan QR links with the camera on your phone** and click the link to take you directly to the video. Try one now for a special message.

CHAPTER 1

Parts of the Machine and Sewing Tools

First, Let's start with 8 things you NEED to get started sewing: your sewing essentials!

1. Sewing Machine - Sewing by hand is wonderful, but if you're looking for speed, a sewing machine is your best friend. It dramatically accelerates your projects by handling the time-consuming tasks at lightning speed, making it 100 times faster than hand sewing. So which sewing machine is best for beginners? See Page 8.

2. Sewing Pins - A slender piece of metal used to hold pattern pieces to fabric, anchor seam allowances as you sew, fit fabric on the body, and secure decorative trims. There are many different pins. They can vary in length and thickness, with colorful ball-shaped glass heads or without. (Learn how to pin your fabric and patterns properly here https://youtu.be/Uj2Vm9UJJ7Y) In some instances you may find sewing clips easier to use to hold your fabric together. (Learn when to use clips vs. pins here https://youtu.be/WO5-ltWbEPE)

3. Needles - A very fine slender piece of metal with a point at one end and a hole or eye for thread at the other, used to join together objects with thread. (Learn which needles to use here https://youtu.be/6js209Uow_s)

4. Thread - The yarn used to combine two or more fabric pieces together in garments, accessories, and other textile products. It can come on different types of spools or a cone. (Learn more about the different types of thread here https://youtu.be/YsID2FKR4Vo)

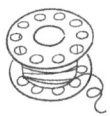

5. Bobbins - The "bobbin" is the thread holder that feeds the thread at the bottom of your machine and appears on the underside of each stitch. Most modern machines either use a class 15 or class 66 bobbin with class 15 being the more common, while older machines more likely use a metal bobbin. To find out which type of bobbin you need for your sewing machine, check your owner's manual or do a quick online search. (Learn how to load your bobbin here https://youtu.be/Gm5vKtaueAQ)

6. Seam Ripper - A small tool to unpick a row of stitches. Replace these occasionally when the knife is dull. (Learn how to take apart seams faster here https://youtu.be/5ZJjRBzYH_U)

7. Tape Measure - A soft and flexible ribbon with linear-measurement markings made mostly from reinforced polyester or fiberglass. The most common length of a measuring tape is 60 inches (or 152 cm), but there are longer tapes for sale, for example, 100 inches long (254 cm) or even longer 120" (304 cm). A tape measure is used primarily for taking body measurements, as well as for drafting patterns, measuring fabric, laying out patterns on fabric, specifying the length of a garment, checking the size of hems, measuring curves and corners, measuring curtains, quilts ... and much more.

8. Sewing Scissors or Fabric Shears - A good pair of scissors is crucial. When scissors are dull, it will be very time consuming to cut even the smallest piece of fabric. Plus, the edges will be jagged. Fabric scissors have a sharper blade with a steeper angle. Normal scissors are typically made from stainless steel, whereas fabric scissors are often made from tough carbon steel that lasts longer and can be sharpened better.

For visual learners, here's

8 things you need to get started sewing and other important sewing tips from Blueprint DIY!

Where can I buy sewing supplies?

Instore - If you want to get supplies on demand, try going to your local fabric store or a big box store like Walmart or Michael's.

Online - To shop from the comfort of your couch, check online retailers like Wawak.com and Amazon. My Amazon storefront has links to all of the products mentioned here.
https://www.amazon.com/shop/blueprintdiy

Shop my favorite sewing products!

Learn more sewing tools and what they're used for.

Pin Cushion - A small stuffed object into which pins are stuck for convenient storage. A pin cushion is a helpful tool to keep your pins organized and at hand when you need them. Now you can get magnetic pin holders that wrap around your arm to keep them close whenever you need them.

Fun Fact: The vintage tomato shaped pin cushions have a little strawberry shaped piece connected with little beads inside meant to sharpen pins.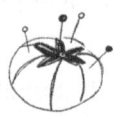

Thimble - A bucket shaped tool designed to protect your finger when pushing a needle through layers of fabric. Can be made of metal, plastic, or leather.

Thread Snips or Nippers - Used to nip the loose threads after you finish stitching. It's faster to grab this tool than reach for scissors.

French Curve or Curved Ruler - A plastic or wooden template having an edge composed of several different curves used for drawing curved lines. Using a French curve allows you to draw a perfectly smooth curve.

Tailor's Chalk - A thin flat piece of hard chalk or soapstone used by tailors and seamstresses for making temporary marks on cloth. You can use chalk to transfer stitch lines, darts, and other markings from your pattern to your fabric.
To save money, try using a sliver of soap left over from bar soap that is typically thown away.

**13 Common Sewing Tools
You Need to Know!**

What Kind of Sewing Machine Do I Need?

The best machine for YOU is the one you'll actually use! You may value simplicity or love bells & whistles. You may be on a tight budget or want something that can stand the test of time. **So, choose a sewing machine based on YOUR needs.**

If you're on a tight budget or you don't know if this sewing thing is right for you, simply choose any sewing machine that has pretty good reviews. As a beginner, a mechanical machine is often sufficient. Choose a machine with basic stitches, easy threading, and reliable performance. Look for features like adjustable stitch length, built-in stitches, and a sturdy build.

Here's a few recommendations in the $100 price range.

Brother LX3817
Janome Easy-to-Use
Brother SM2700

Best Sewing Machines for beginners under $100

If you want something that's going to grow with you on your sewing journey look for these two main features: a back stitch and a one-step buttonhole. Two additional features that make life easier are speed control and needle auto up/down. Check the glossary for the meanings to these terms. My favorite sewing machines in this category also tend to be pretty tough because I have no patience for a finicky sewing machine. Here's my favorites for the impatient beginner.

One step buttonhole and back stitch:
Janome 1522
Brother Strong & Tough
Singer Heavy Duty 4432

Also have speed control and needle auto up/down:
Bernette B37
Singer Heavy Duty 6800c
Husqvarna Viking Emerald 118

Beginner Sewing Machines that were made to last

Don't forget about used sewing machines!

If you're willing to do a little searching, purchasing a used sewing machine can be the ultimate jackpot. Vintage sewing machines with their all metal bodies were built to sew through tough materials and made to last forever. Scoring one of these coveted machines could be a dream come true if you're willing to get it serviced by a sewing machine technician.

Some places to search for used sewing machines are:
Thrift Stores
Goodwill.com
Facebook Marketplace
Ebay
Craigslist

Don't forget to ask relatives and neighbors. There are probably enough used sewing machines currently sitting in boxes and attics for every single person looking for one. Your family members may have this treasure throve just waiting for you. I just brought my grandmother's 1920s Singer on a Southwest flight home to Houston from my parents' home in Chicago for FREE!

Parts of the Sewing Machine

Understand key parts like the needle, presser foot, bobbin, and feed dogs. Knowing these parts helps you troubleshoot and use your machine effectively.

1. Power Switch
2. Hand Wheel
3. Bobbin Winder Pin
4. Bobbin Winder Stop
5. Spool Pin
6. Spool Pin Cap
7. Bobbin Winder Tension Disk
8. Thread Guide
9. Tension Control
10. Take-Up Lever
11. Needle Clamp
12. Needle
13. Presser Foot
14. Feed Dogs
15. Presser Lever
16. Needle Plate
17. Bobbin Case
18. Stitch Selector
19. Stitch Length Selector
20. Reverse Stitch Lever
21. Foot pedal

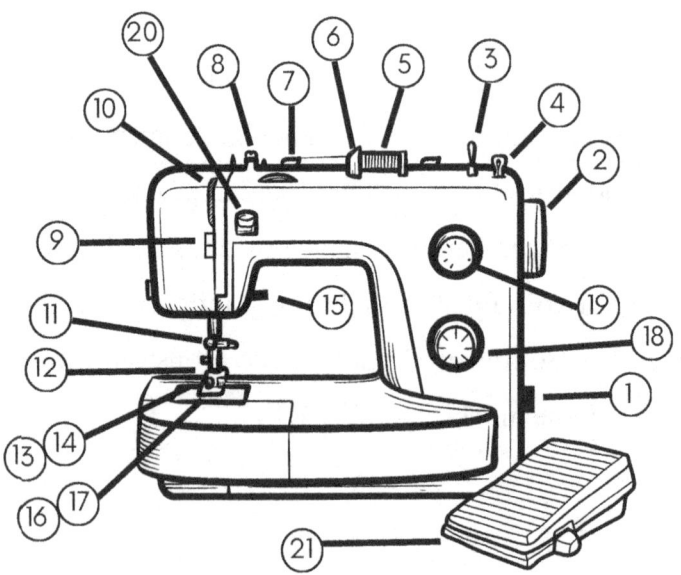

1. Power Switch - button on the right side of the sewing machine that causes the sewing machine to come on

2. Hand Wheel - the round wheel typically located at the upper right of the sewing machine to manually advance the stitch (The hand wheel or balance wheel should only be manually turned towards you in the direction that advances the sewing machine —*unless the thread gets stuck then rock the handwheel back and forth to release the stuck fabric*)

3. Bobbin Winder Pin - used to hold and wind an empty bobbin

4. Bobbin Winder Stop - stops the bobbin winding when the bobbin reaches its optimum capacity

5. Spool Pin - used to hold the spool of thread, can be horizontal or vertical

6. Spool Pin Cap - designed to keep the thread spool on the machine as you sew (To keep your thread from catching on the spool cap and breaking, match the size of the spool cap with the size of the thread spool)

7. Bobbin Winder Tension Disk - small metal disc helps to keep the thread taut as you wind a bobbin

8. Thread Guide - a device that has a loop or an eye, for guiding the thread when it is necessary to change the direction at any point between the spool and the needle

9. Tension Control - putting varying amounts of tension (or strength) on the threads they control to form a strong, balanced stitch

10. Take-Up Lever - pulls the thread off the spool and helps supply an even feed of thread to your needle. The take-up lever is the metal lever (looks like a hook) that is on top of your machine and moves up and down while you sew. Your needle has to be all the way up to see it

11. Needle Clamp - holds sewing machine needle in place

12. Sewing Machine Needle - a specialized needle for use in a sewing machine (eye or hole is close to the point as opposed to hand sewing needles where the eye is on the opposite end from the point.)

13. Presser Foot - an attachment used with sewing machines to hold fabric flat as it is fed through the machine and stitched

14. Feed Dogs - the little razor teeth underneath the presser foot on your sewing machine that feed your fabric evenly through the machine (extremely important because they help us produce perfectly spaced, even stitches whenever we sew). In some machines, these can be lowered for free motion quilting.

15. Presser Lever - (or Presser Bar) raises and lowers the presser foot to place pressure on the feed-dog so that the fabric placed between the feed dog and the presser foot does not shift. Presser lever should always be in the down position while sewing

16. Needle Plate - a metal plate that sits below the presser foot with a small opening that allows the bobbin thread to come out and the needle to pass through to make stitches

17. Bobbin Case - holds the bobbin in the sewing machine so that the machine stitches can be formed

18. Stitch Selector - allows you to switch between stitch styles such as straight stitch and zig zag stitch

19. Stitch Length Selector - indicates the length of a single stitch in millimetres (standard is between 2.5 to 3) When sewing decorative stitches you'll also need to adjust the stitch width selector to choose the width of your decorative stitch

20. Reverse Stitch Lever - (or back stitch) button that allows your sewing machine to sew backwards to lock stitches in place, typically used at the beginning and end of a stitch

21. Foot pedal - sits on the floor connected to your sewing machine with a cord and tells your sewing machine when to go and when to stop

Need to see the parts in action? Learn the parts of your sewing machine here: https://youtu.be/0ZE3tkjk7AI

CHAPTER 2

How to Set Up Your Sewing Machine

Setting up your sewing
machine step-by-step

Your sewing machine likely came with several ways to show you how to thread it. There could be a manual, a CD, and/or a **quick-start guide**. Follow the instructions thoroughly because proper threading is crucial for smooth sewing. If you purchased a used machine without a manual, all is not lost. Do a quick online search with the name of the sewing machine and the word "manual" afterwards. Even some vintage sewing machine manuals can be found in pdf format online. However, most home sewing machines thread in a similar manner, so let's get to it.

How to Wind the Bobbin

Place the thread on the spool pin (5) and secure it with the spool cap (6) if the spool pin is horizontal. Guide it around and under the tension disc (7).

Place the thread through the tiny hole on top of the bobbin from the underside and load the bobbin onto the bobbin winder pin (3).

Push the bobbin winder pin to the right towards the bobbin winder stop (4) and press the foot pedal (21) while holding the thread up and away from the bobbin. After the bobbin base is covered with thread, cut the thread coming out of the top of the bobbin and continue winding until it stops or starts to stutter.

Before Threading Your Machine

Make sure your sewing machine is off. Roll the hand wheel (2) towards you until the needle (12) is at its highest position.

How to Thread a Sewing Machine

Put the thread on the spool pin (5) and secure it with the spool cap (6) if the spool pin is horizontal. No spool cap is required for vertical spool pins.

Pull the thread to the thread guide (8) over to the left. Pay attention to the markings on your sewing machine. Most modern sewing machines guide you on threading the machine with arrows or numbers in step order.

Now bring the thread from the thread guide (8) over the top of the machine (10) down the front of the machine and back up behind or through the take-up lever (10).

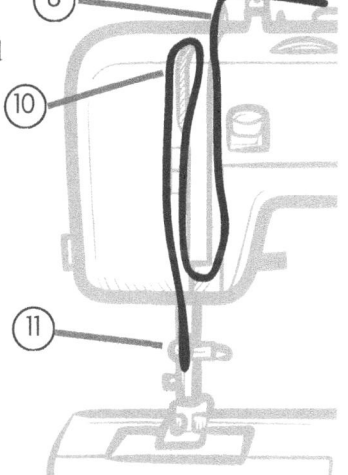

Now bring the thread down behind the thread guide attached right below the needle clamp (11). This is a step that many beginners miss because there's no way to mark it on the machine. Now cut the tip of your thread to make sure it's not frayed and thread it through the needle from front to back going away from you.

How to Load the Bobbin

Insert the bobbin into the bobbin case (17) with the thread going in a counter clockwise direction (check your manual to verify thread direction). This prevents thread jams.

Guide the thread under the metal notch and to the left side. This step will vary depending on whether your sewing machine has a drop-in bobbin or vertical bobbin. (Learn how to load both types of bobbins here https://youtu.be/Gm5vKtaueAQ)

Learn how to load both types here

How to Pull Up the Bobbin Thread

Hold the thread coming through the needle with your left hand very loosely while turning the hand wheel towards you to lower the needle below the needle plate.

Continue to turn the handwheel to raise the needle back up to it's highest position. Then pull on the thread being held in your left hand until you see a loop of the bobbin thread coming up through the needle plate. Pull the loop so that the bobbin thread comes the rest of the way up. Put both threads under the presser foot and to the back. You're now ready to sew. If you need more help with this step check out the video above.

Types of Needles

Different projects require different needles. Sewing machine needles are different than hand sewing needles. The eye or hole of a sewing machine needle is close to the point as opposed to hand sewing needles where the eye is on the opposite end from the point. Impatient beginners should **start with a pack of universal needles** because they work for most fabrics. As you progress to more detailed projects follow this helpful guide to know which needle to use on your project.

MACHINE NEEDLE SIZE GUIDE

60/8	Very fine fabric like lingerie, silk and fine lace.
70/10	Net, Chiffon Lingerie, silk and cotton
75/11	Voile, Chiffon, Organza, Denim, Satin, Sweater, Silk, Dress Shirt, Lycra, Spandex
80/12	Tricot, Silks, Canvas
90/14	Syn Velvets, Poplin, Linen, Light Wool, Jersey, Muslin
100/16	Cord, Denim, Heavy Suiting, Corduroy
110/18	Heavy Denim, Leather, Upholstery Fabric, Faux Fur
120/20	Super heavy fabrics: Cord, Denim, Heavy Suiting

TYPES OF SEWING MACHINE NEEDLES

Universal - for most fabrics

Jersey/Ballpoint - for jersey knits

Stretch - for stretchy fabrics

Jeans/Denim - for denim fabrics

Microtex/Sharp - for top stitching

Leather - to sew leather and suede

Self threading - has a notch to allow easy threading

Types of Needles

HAND SEWING NEEDLE GUIDE

SHARPS - General purpose needle with sharp point for sewing and applique

DARNERS - Long needle with sharp point and long eye used for mending

EMBROIDERY - Sharp needle with long eye for smocking, heirloom sewing, embroidery and crewel

MILLINERS - Long needle with small round eye for gathering, pleating, basting and millinery work

TAPESTRY - Large-eyed needle with a blunt point for cross-stitch, needlepoint and for stitching knitted items

Types of Thread

Don't get intimidated by the amount of thread in the store! If you are just getting into sewing, **just grab some all purpose thread**. This thread will work for most of your beginner projects. As you progress, here's a helpful guide to know what these different threads are used for.

All-Purpose Thread - Polyester thread that works for most sewing projects, including garments and general-purpose sewing. It's the go-to thread for beginners because it is versatile and widely available in many colors and sizes.

Button and Craft Thread - Thicker thread specifically designed for sewing on buttons, especially on heavier garments like blazers. It's also used in certain craft projects where additional strength is needed.

Embroidery Thread - Thinner and shinier, embroidery thread is used for machine embroidery to create detailed and vibrant designs. It's designed to work smoothly in embroidery machines, avoiding clogging.

Jean Thread - Thicker thread used for sewing denim projects. It's durable and comes in traditional denim colors, but it may require adjustments to your sewing machine settings for best results.

Metallic Thread - Used for decorative stitching, metallic thread adds a shiny, eye-catching effect to garments. It's best for top-stitching on thinner fabrics and can be delicate, requiring careful handling.

Upholstery Thread - Similar to jean thread but even stronger, upholstery thread is used for sewing heavy-duty items like upholstery and heavyweight curtains. It's durable and designed to hold up under stress.

These thread types provide a wide range of options for different sewing needs, from basic garment construction to decorative and heavy-duty projects.

The Right Thread for your Sewing Project

CHAPTER 3

Practicing - How to Sew

Learn to Sew in 20 minutes

Now you're ready to sew.

Turn your sewing machine on (1), place your fabric underneath the presser foot (13), put the presser foot down with the presser lever (15), gently press the foot pedal (21), and gently hold the fabric to guide its direction.

Important Things to Remember!
Always put your presser foot down before starting to sew. If not, the underside of your stitch will be very loose and your thread may jam.

Practice These Skills

Straight stitch - The most basic machine stitch, that produces a single row of straight, even stitches. It's used to construct a garment and for topstitching. The straight stitch will be denoted by a dashed line on your stitch selector (18). Practice changing the stitch length (19) for a longer or shorter stitch.

Back stitch - the reverse stitch on your sewing machine will have a turning arrow symbol ↑ going either up or down ↓. Start by sewing about 1/2 inch forward, then press and hold your back stitch button (20) while sewing and your machine will sew backwards. Release the back stitch button and your machine will start sewing forward again.

Zig Zag Stitch - Z-shaped stitch that can be used on knits, stretch fabrics, to sew buttonholes and as a finish for raw edges. Practice making different size zig zag stitches by changing the stitch length and stitch width.

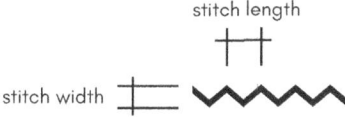

Practice These Shapes
Use practice sheets in the back of this book to learn stitching straight lines and curves. Consistent practice improves your control over the fabric. Set your sewing machine to a straight stitch and practice controlling the direction of what you're sewing.

Practice Cutting
A jagged edge makes it difficult to sew straight seams, which can cause uneven, inconsistent stitching and frustration during sewing. Save your sanity and **learn to cut straight**. Use sharp scissors for clean cuts. Lay the fabric flat and cut slowly along the pattern lines. If you have trouble cutting straight, here's a few tips to help.
- Iron out wrinkles - Wrinkled fabric cannot be cut straight.
- Pin the fabric - especially slippery fabrics, to prevent them from shifting during cutting. If using a pattern, pin it securely to the fabric.
- Mark the fabric - Use a ruler or a straight edge to mark a straight line on the fabric. You can use tools like heat-

erasable markers for precise markings. This helps guide your scissors for a straight cut.
- Use Long Even Strokes - Cut using the entire blade of your scissors, not just the tips. Open the scissors wide, and take long, smooth strokes to avoid jagged edges.

How to Cut Straight Step-by-Step

Practice Pinning

Pinning keeps fabric layers together. When pinning fabric together or patterns to fabric, **push the pin through the layers and back up to the surface**. Then ensure that the layers are flat and not bunched up or puckered. Make sure the head of your pins do not cross over the edge of the pattern while cutting so that you don't ruin a good pair of sewing scissors by accidentally cutting a metal pin. When pinning fabric edge for sewing, place pins perpendicular to the seam line to avoid sewing over them.

How to Pin Fabric Step-by-Step

CHAPTER 4

How To Care For Your Sewing Machine

Sewing Machine Care

Proper maintenance can prevent many of the issues that might cause frustration or halt your sewing projects altogether. Plus, knowing how to troubleshoot common problems will save you time and keep your creativity flowing. Your sewing machine needs a little love and attention to perform at its best. Regular maintenance not only extends the life of the machine but also ensures smooth stitching every time you sew.

1. Cleaning Your Sewing Machine
- Frequency: Aim to clean your machine every 4-6 hours of sewing (or after each project if it's a big one).
- Tools: Use a small, soft brush or a vacuum with a narrow nozzle to remove dust and lint from the bobbin case, feed dogs, and around the needle area.
- Oil Your Machine: Some machines have oiling points. If your machine requires oiling, make sure to use sewing machine oil (never use regular oil). Follow your machine's manual for guidance on where to apply the oil.
- Needle & Presser Foot: Wipe these parts with a soft cloth regularly.

2. Changing the Needle
- When to Change: Change your needle regularly, especially

when you notice problems with stitching or fabric. Needles wear out after 6-8 hours of use or when you start working with thicker fabrics like denim.
- Needle Type: Make sure you're using the right type of needle for the fabric you're sewing. For example, use a ballpoint needle for knits, a denim needle for thicker fabrics, and a universal needle for most basic projects.
- How to Change: Loosen the needle screw at the needle clamp (11) with the screwdriver provided with your machine, then slide the old needle out and replace it with a new one. Be sure the flat side of the needle faces the back.

3. Cleaning the Bobbin Case
- Why It's Important: A clean bobbin case ensures that the thread feeds smoothly and that your stitches stay even.
- How to Clean: Remove the bobbin, and use a brush to remove any lint or dust. Be gentle so you don't damage any parts of the bobbin assembly.

4. Checking the Feed Dogs
- What They Do: The feed dogs grip and move the fabric through the machine while sewing. Over time, they can get clogged with fabric lint or dust.
- How to Clean: Remove the throat plate by removing screws (if possible), and gently clean the area with a brush to clear any buildup around the feed dogs.

Final Tips for Sewing Machine Longevity
- Always unplug your machine when you're not using it, especially if you're cleaning or changing needles.
- Avoid sewing over pins, as this can break your needle and damage the machine.
- Keep your sewing area free of dust and lint, especially around the machine's internal components.

By regularly cleaning and troubleshooting your sewing machine, you'll prevent small issues from turning into big problems and keep your machine running smoothly for years to come.

Common Sewing Machine Problems

Learn to troubleshoot issues like thread jams, skipped stitches, and tension problems. Understanding common problems helps you solve them quickly.

Quick Guide: Most sewing machine problems can be solved by proper threading, changing the needle, using the correct needle, adjusting tension, and ensuring that no threads are caught in the bobbin case.

1. Thread Bunching (Bird's Nest) Under Fabric - the thread forms a messy clump under the fabric.
- You may have sewn the stitch with the presser foot up. Try the stitch again with the presser foot down.

- If that wasn't the case try rethreading both the upper thread and bobbin, ensuring the thread passes through all guides correctly.
- Check that the bobbin is wound evenly.
- Adjust the upper thread tension (usually by loosening it slightly). Typical tension should be between 3 and 5.

2. Skipped Stitches - the machine skips stitches, leaving gaps in the seam.
- Your needle may be bent. Replace the needle with a new one and ensure it's the correct type for your fabric.
- Rethread the machine, making sure the thread is seated correctly in the tension disks.
- Check that the needle is inserted correctly, pushed all the way up into the needle clamp (11) and fully tightened.
- Clean the machine, especially around the feed dogs (14) and bobbin area, to remove lint and debris.

3. Needle Breaking - the needle breaks frequently.
- Your needle may be too thin for the fabric you're sewing. See needle guide on page 19 to ensure correct size for type of fabric. Check that the needle is properly inserted and not bent or damaged.
- Avoid pulling fabric while sewing; let the feed dogs move it.
- Ensure the presser foot and needle are correctly aligned.
- Ensure needle plate is not bent. If so, you can order a new one or remove and hammer it back in place with a mallet.

4. Machine Jamming - the sewing machine jams, and the handwheel won't turn.
- Turn off the machine and remove the fabric, thread, and bobbin. Remove any trapped threads or lint from the bobbin area.
- Check for any fabric stuck in the feed dogs.
- Rethread the machine and correctly insert the bobbin.

5. Uneven or Loose Stitches - stitches appear loose or uneven.
- Adjust the thread tension settings. Try moving the tension dial slightly higher or lower and test on a scrap piece of fabric to find the right tension.
- Ensure that both the upper and lower threads are threaded correctly.
- Use the correct thread type and size for your fabric.

6. Machine Not Feeding Fabric - the fabric isn't moving forward while sewing.
- Ensure the feed dogs are raised (not lowered for free-motion sewing). Clean the feed dogs to remove any lint or debris.
- Check that the presser foot is down.
- Use the correct presser foot for the fabric and stitch type.

7. Sewing Machine Making Strange Noises - Unusual sounds can be caused by the sewing machine being too dry (needs oiling) or the needle hitting something it shouldn't (like a pin or fabric catch).

- Clean and oil the machine according to the manufacturer's instructions.
- Check that all screws and parts are tightened and secure.
- Remove any jammed fabric, thread, or lint from the machine. Check for any obstructions, like pins or caught threads, and remove them.
- Ensure the needle is not bent and is properly installed.

8. Bobbin Thread Not Catching - the needle doesn't pick up the bobbin thread. This can happen if the machine is threaded incorrectly, the needle is bent, or the timing is off.
- Rethread the machine, ensuring the bobbin is correctly inserted.
- Check the needle for proper insertion and ensure it's the right type. Check that the needle is not bent or damaged and replace it if needed.
- Manually rotate the handwheel to ensure the needle is moving properly.
- Clean the bobbin case and surrounding area for loose threads or obstructions.
- If the problem persists, the machine's timing may need adjustment by a professional.

9. Fabric Puckering - the fabric wrinkles or puckers along the seam. This can occur if the fabric isn't feeding through the machine evenly, often caused by improper tension or the wrong presser foot.

- Adjust the tension settings, loosening the upper thread tension. A higher thread tension equals a looser stitch.
- Use the correct needle size and type for your fabric.
- Try using a stabilizer or interfacing with lightweight or delicate fabrics.
- Reduce the presser foot pressure if your machine has this adjustment.
- Use the correct presser foot for the fabric you're working with (e.g., use a walking foot for thick or slippery fabrics).
- Make sure the feed dogs are raised, and the fabric is being guided evenly.

10. Sewing Machine Not Turning On - you're pressing the power button on the machine and nothing is happening.
- Check that the power cord is securely plugged in and that the outlet is working. Press the foot pedal to see if normal operation occurs because it may just be a blown light bulb.
- Inspect the foot pedal connection.
- Look for any blown fuses or tripped breakers in the machine or your home electrical system.
- If the machine still doesn't turn on, it may require professional servicing.

11. Thread Keeps Breaking - This often happens when the thread is too old or poor quality, the needle is too small for the thread, or the machine is incorrectly threaded.

- Use high-quality thread and check the expiration date on your thread spool.
- Ensure the needle size is compatible with the thread you're using (e.g., thicker thread needs a larger needle).
- Re-thread the machine, checking that the thread isn't twisted or tangled.

12. Thread Is Tangling in the Bobbin Area - Tangles usually occur when the bobbin is wound incorrectly or the tension is too tight.
- Ensure that the needle is at the highest position before removing fabric after a stitch.
- Rewind the bobbin, ensuring it's wound evenly and not overfilled or loose.
- Clean the bobbin case to remove any lint or debris.
- Adjust the tension of the upper thread, ensuring it's not too tight.

13. Machine Runs Too Slowly or Won't Start - A slow machine could be due to a motor issue, a jam, or the machine not being plugged in properly.
- Check that the foot pedal and machine power cord are securely connected.
- Turn the machine off, remove the fabric, and check for any jams in the needle area or bobbin.
- If the motor is still not running, it may require professional servicing.

14. Machine is Sticking or Jamming at the Needle - This could be because the needle is too thin for the fabric, or there's fabric caught around the needle mechanism.
- Use the correct needle size for your fabric.
- Check for any fabric stuck around the needle or presser foot, and clear it away.

Additional Pro Tips
- Test Sew on Scraps: Before working on your actual project, test the machine on a fabric scrap to make sure everything is running smoothly.
- Read the Manual: Familiarize yourself with your machine's manual. It's full of troubleshooting tips and diagrams that can help solve a lot of problems.
- Don't Force It: If the machine is not working, don't force it. Check for jams, issues with the needle, or bobbin, and make adjustments before trying again.
- Schedule Professional Maintenance: If you encounter persistent issues or if your machine is making odd noises or is acting up, consider having it serviced by a professional once a year.

By being proactive with care and knowing how to troubleshoot common issues, you'll keep your sewing machine running like a dream and avoid interruptions in your creative process.

CHAPTER 5

What If I Mess Up?

Tips to Keep You Going!

Take a Deep Breath & Step Back - Mistakes happen to everyone —even the pros! When you realize something didn't go as planned, take a moment to breathe. Step back and give yourself a minute to reset. *It's ok to throw a fit, just put the project down first.*

Embrace the Learning Curve - Since you're impatient, I'll spare you the speech about your mistakes being stepping stones to greatness. Mistakes happen. You're doing amazing just by sticking with it!

Analyze & Adjust - Look at what went wrong and why. Did the fabric slip? Did you sew the wrong pieces together? Whatever it was, figure out how it happened and how you can avoid it next time.

Seam Rippers Are Your Best Friend - I know we all dread them, but put on your favorite show and sit on the couch and get to picking. It's better to take the time to fix a mistake than to rush through it. And hey, ripping out seams is a skill too—one that gets better with practice!

Get Creative with Your Fix - Sometimes, a mistake can lead to a happy accident. Can you turn that oops into a new design feature? Maybe that uneven hem can be turned into a chic asymmetrical look, or that misplaced seam can become a decorative stitch. Be open to where your creativity can take you!

Two of my "Oops" Projects Turned Great

Ask for Help - You're not in this alone! Whether it's through my tutorials, a sewing community, or even reaching out to me directly, there's always someone who's been there and can offer advice or encouragement. Don't be shy about asking for help. I have a whole Facebook group dedicated to sharing our sewing wins and woes. Check it out here https://www.facebook.com/groups/2181810768549341

Celebrate Small Wins - Every stitch, every cut, and every seam—whether perfect or not—is a victory. You're a baby sewist and expect to sew like a pro? Celebrate the progress you're making, no matter how small it may seem. You're learning and growing with every project, and that's something to be proud of!

When to Give Up - If a project takes you to the point where you're ready to give up sewing, **put it in time-out**. After completing other projects, perhaps they'll give you the skills needed to complete that one. And if all else fails, buy an empty floor pouf or dog bed and stuff all your failed projects inside so they are still useful in the end.

Keep pushing forward, and remember—every great sewist has a pile of "oops" projects in their closet. You've got this!

How to Seam Rip

Use a seam ripper to carefully undo mistakes. Be careful not to cut the fabric while removing stitches.

Learn faster ways to rip seams

Straight Stitches - Place the sharp end of the seam ripper under each stitch and push to cut the thread. Once one stitch is cut, the next can be pulled free by inserting the seam ripper and pulling with the dull edge. Keep doing this carefully until the stitch is removed.

Chain Stitches - Start by finding one end of the chain stitch. Pick at the thread until you can loosen it and pull. If it doesn't unravel smoothly, switch to the other end and repeat.

Serged Seams - Focus on the side with the "loopies" or teardrop shapes. Use the seam ripper to remove the stitches between the loops. After removing enough stitches, you should be able to pull the thread out in a single motion.

Tips for Faster Seam Ripping
Instead of removing stitches one by one, use the small ball end of the seam ripper. Insert the ball under the seam and slide the seam ripper along to quickly cut the stitches. The ball end was intended to help separate the fabric and glide through the seam.

Use Special Tools - Don't hesitate to use specialized tools like a surgical seam ripper or a razor for tough or thick seams, as they speed up the process considerably.

Gentle Pulling - When pulling on chain stitches or serged seams, do so gently to avoid re-knotting the thread or damaging the fabric.

Take Your Time on Delicate Fabrics - Although the focus is on speed, ensure you're careful with delicate fabrics to avoid causing unnecessary damage.

Practice Makes Perfect - The more you practice these techniques, the quicker and more efficient you'll become at seam ripping, which is crucial in sewing and upcycling projects.

CHAPTER 6

How to Measure Yourself

How to Measure Yourself for
Online Shopping and Sewing

Getting accurate measurements is the foundation of creating garments that fit perfectly. Whether you're making something for yourself or someone else, proper measurements are key to a successful sewing project. Here's a helpful guide to aid in the process.

How to Measure Yourself Accurately

Use a flexible measuring tape. Stand straight, measure snugly but not tightly, and record your measurements. Keep reading for a more detailed explanation.

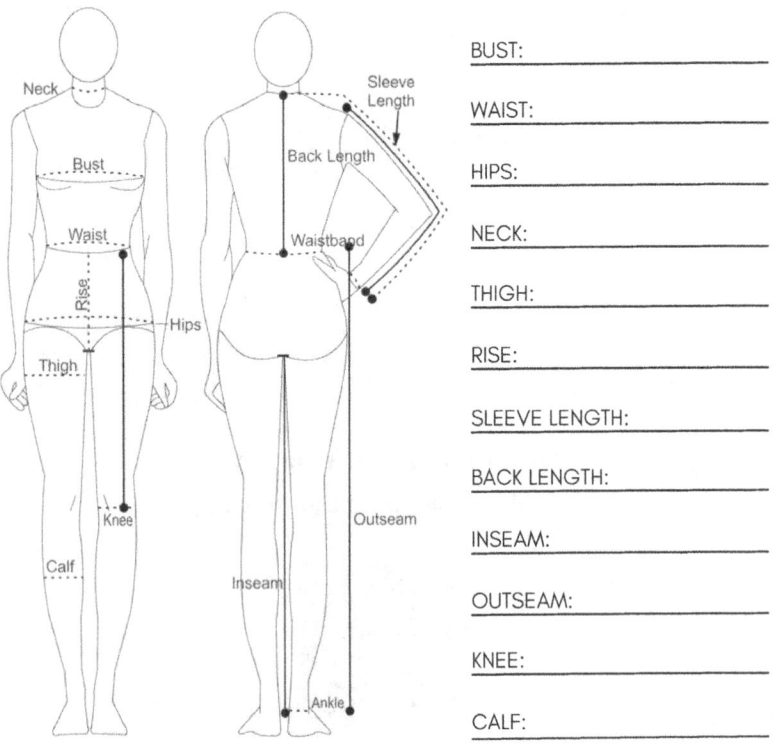

BUST: _____

WAIST: _____

HIPS: _____

NECK: _____

THIGH: _____

RISE: _____

SLEEVE LENGTH: _____

BACK LENGTH: _____

INSEAM: _____

OUTSEAM: _____

KNEE: _____

CALF: _____

Tools You'll Need
- Flexible measuring tape
- A mirror (preferably full-length)
- A pen and paper (or your phone) to jot down measurements
- A friend to help (optional but helpful for accuracy)

Preparation
Wear Fitted Clothing - Wear something close-fitting or just your undergarments so the measurements reflect your body shape accurately. When making formal attire, wear the undergarments that will be worn with the garment to ensure a proper fit.

Stand Naturally - Stand in your natural posture. Don't suck in your stomach or puff out your chest. You want the measurements to reflect your true body shape.

Key Measurements to Take
Bust - Wrap the measuring tape around the fullest part of your bust, making sure it's parallel to the floor and snug but not tight. Write down the measurement.

Waist - Locate your natural waistline, which is typically the narrowest part of your torso. Measure around this area, keeping the tape parallel to the floor. Don't suck in your stomach; relax and take a natural measurement.

Hips - Measure around the fullest part of your hips and

buttocks, keeping the tape snug and parallel to the floor. This is usually around 7-9 inches below your waistline.

Back Length, Shoulder to Waist - Start from the highest point on your shoulder and measure down to your natural waistline. This measurement is crucial for ensuring that tops and dresses fit well in the torso.

Shoulder or Back Width - Measure across your back from one shoulder blade to the other. This is especially important for fitted tops and jackets.

Arm Length - With your arm relaxed by your side and slightly bent, measure from the top of your shoulder (where you feel your shoulder bone) down to your wrist following the bend of your elbow.

Inseam - Measure from the crotch down to the ankle (or wherever you want the hem of your pants to end). Stand straight and ask for help if needed to get an accurate measurement.

Outseam - Measure from your waist (at the side of your body) down to your desired hem length for skirts or pants.

Thigh - Measure around the fullest part of your thigh, which is generally a few inches below the hip joint. This measurement could also be from the waist to the thigh for a mini skirt length.

Calf - If you're making fitted pants or leggings, measure around the fullest part of your calf. This could also be from the waist to the calf for a midi skirt length.

Neck Circumference - Measure around the base of your neck, where a collar would sit.

Tips for Accurate Measuring

Use a Mirror - If measuring alone, use a mirror to ensure the tape measure is level and not twisted.

Measure Twice - Double-check each measurement for accuracy before writing it down.

Avoid Over-tightening - The tape should be snug but not tight. You should be able to slip a finger underneath the tape comfortably.

Don't Assume - your measurements from last month may not be the same as today so quickly re-check these often to make sure your finished garments fit like a dream—it's worth it!

CHAPTER 7

How to Read a Pattern

How to Choose & Read Sewing Patterns

Reading a sewing pattern might seem like deciphering a secret code at first, but once you know how to read them, you'll unlock the door to endless creative possibilities. Sewing patterns are like blueprints for your projects—they guide you through the process from start to finish. Here's a step-by-step guide to help you navigate your first pattern with confidence.

Understanding the Pattern Envelope

The pattern envelope is your first introduction to the project. Here's what you'll find on it:

Front - The front usually shows the finished look of the garment or item, often in multiple styles or variations. This is a great way to visualize what your finished project will look like.

Back - The back is where the technical details live. You'll see:
- Sizing Information: Most patterns cover multiple sizes. You'll need to take your measurements and compare them to the size chart to find the right size for you. Sometimes this information will be found on the flap.
- Fabric Suggestions: This section suggests the types of fabric that work best with the pattern. Stick to these for your first time through to ensure the best results.
- Notions: This includes any additional materials you'll need like zippers, buttons, or elastic.
- Fabric Requirements: This tells you how much fabric you'll need based on your size and the width of the fabric.

The Impatient Beginner's Guide to Sewing

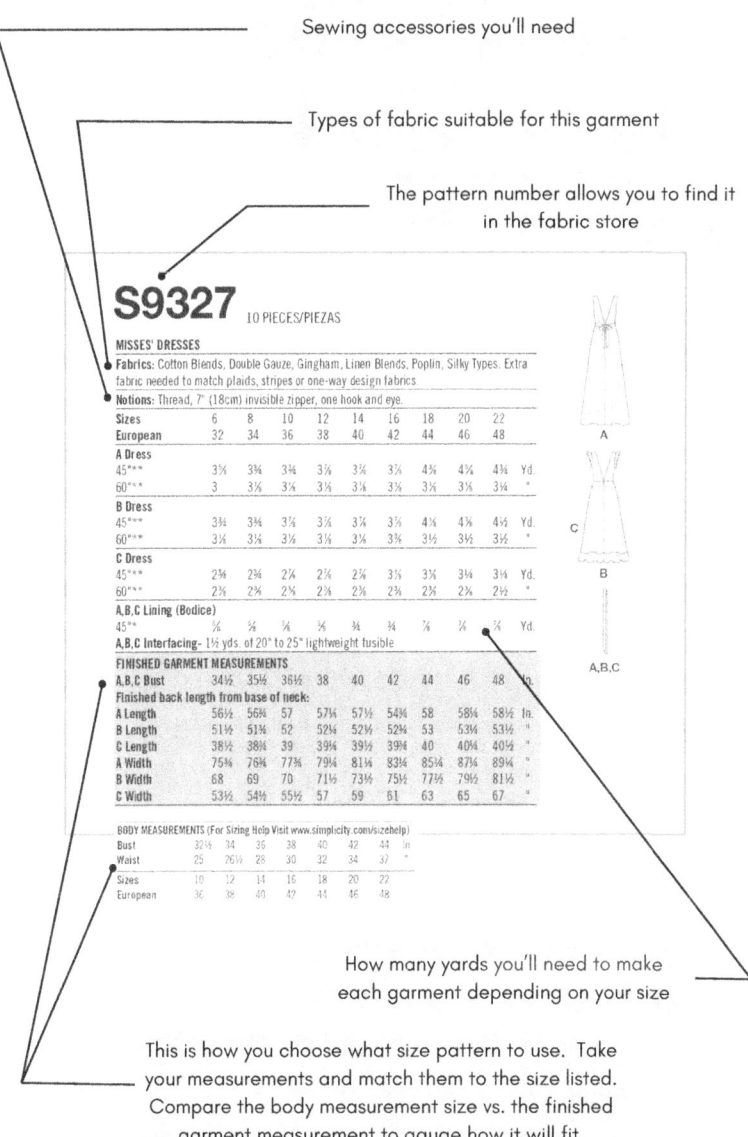

Pattern Sizes are not the same as retail! You will often be a much bigger size in patterns. Don't take it personally. It's like comparing men's shoe sizes to women's. It's just a different metric.

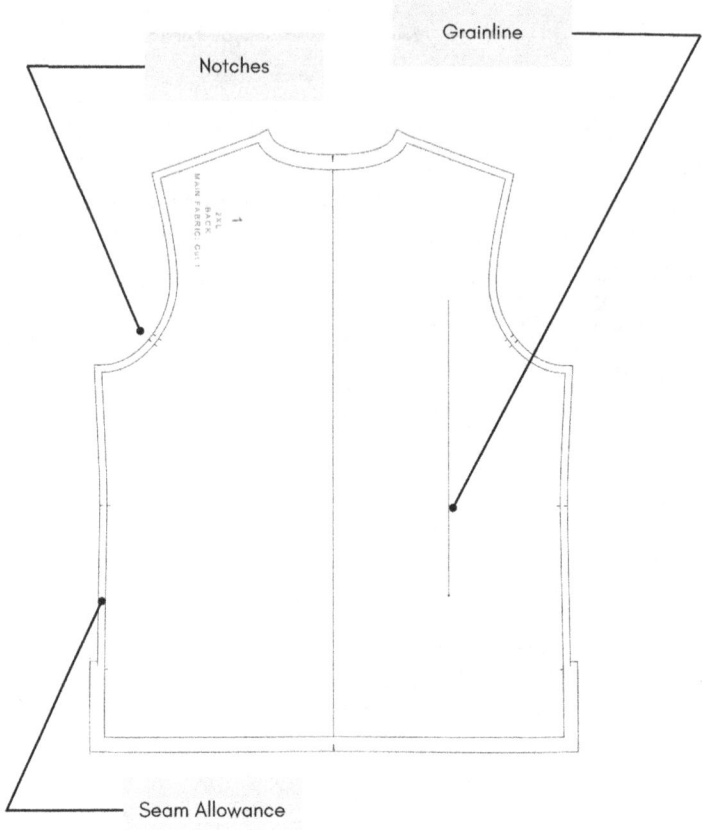

Pattern Pieces

Inside the envelope, you'll find sheets of tissue paper with printed pattern pieces. Each piece corresponds to a part of your project (like a sleeve, bodice, or pocket). Here's how to approach them:

- Identify Your Pieces: The pattern will have a key or legend, usually on the instruction sheet, that tells you which pieces you need for the version you're making. Each piece is numbered and labeled.

- Grainline: Each pattern piece will have a line marked with arrows, called the grainline. When you place your pattern piece on your fabric, align this line parallel to the fabric's selvage edge (the tightly woven edge that doesn't fray). This ensures your project will hang correctly.
- Notches and Markings: These are small triangles or other shapes along the edges of your pattern pieces. They're used to match up seams and other important points during construction. Mark them on your fabric with chalk or a fabric pen.

Instruction Sheet

The instruction sheet is your roadmap through the sewing process. Here's how to follow it:
- Layout Diagrams: These diagrams show you how to place your pattern pieces on your fabric. Pay attention to the diagrams that match your fabric width and the view you're making. Proper layout saves fabric and ensures your pieces are cut on the right grain.

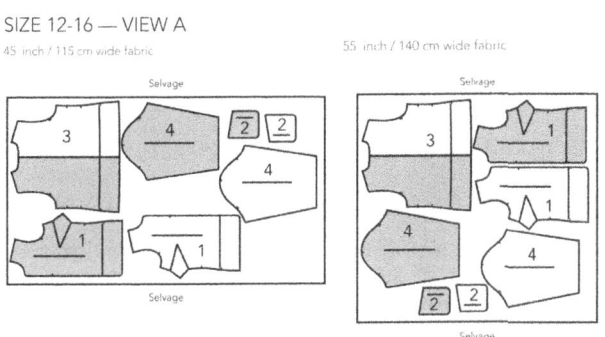

- Sewing Steps: The instructions will guide you step by step through assembling your project. Read through the entire instruction sheet before you start sewing so you understand the overall process. Some instructions may seem confusing at first glance, but they'll make more sense as you start working through them.

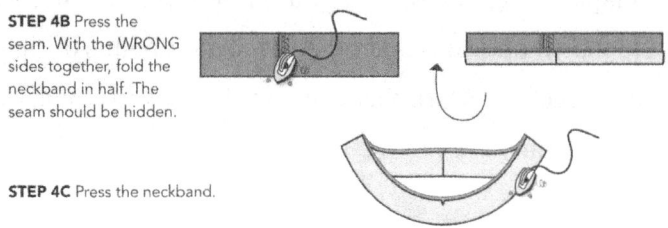

STEP 4B Press the seam. With the WRONG sides together, fold the neckband in half. The seam should be hidden.

STEP 4C Press the neckband.

- Seam Allowances: The seam allowance is the space between the edge of the fabric and the stitching line, usually 5/8 inch (1.5 cm) unless otherwise stated. This is included in most patterns, but double-check to be sure.

Cutting Your Fabric

- Prepare Your Fabric: Pre-wash and press your fabric to eliminate any shrinkage or wrinkles before cutting.
- Pin Your Pattern Pieces: Use pins or pattern weights to secure your pattern pieces to the fabric. Cut carefully around the edges with sharp fabric scissors.
- Transfer Markings: Use chalk, a fabric marker, or tailor's tacks to transfer any important markings like darts, buttonholes, or notches from the pattern to your fabric.

Assembling Your Project

Once everything is cut and marked, follow the sewing instructions step by step. It's a good idea to check each step off as you go. Take your time and don't rush—careful assembly leads to a polished finished product.

Final Touches

After sewing, press your seams as instructed, and add any final details like buttons, zippers, or hems. And there you have it—your guide to reading and understanding a sewing pattern! The more patterns you use, the more familiar and intuitive the process will become. Soon, you'll be confidently tackling projects of all shapes and sizes!

Where to Find Patterns

Now that you're familiar with how to read a sewing pattern, let's talk about where you can find them. The good news is, you have tons of options! Whether you're shopping in-store or searching online, there's a pattern out there for every project and style. Plus, you can even find free patterns that allow you to try new designs without spending a dime.

Fabric Stores

Most fabric stores carry a variety of sewing patterns. You'll find big brand names like Simplicity, McCall's, Butterick, and

Vogue Patterns. These brands offer a wide range of designs, from simple beginner-friendly projects to more complex garments. Look for large binders or pattern books in the store that contain images of all the patterns available from these brands. You can flip through them, jot down the pattern numbers you like, and then search the drawers in the store for the corresponding pattern envelopes.

Online Pattern Shops
If you prefer shopping from the comfort of your own home, the internet is a treasure trove of patterns. Here are some popular places to start:
- Indie Designers - Independent designers are booming in the sewing community, offering unique and modern patterns. Websites like Etsy, IndieSew, and Sew Over It feature a plethora of indie patterns that you can purchase and download instantly.
- Big Brand Websites - The major brands like Simplicity and McCall's also have their own online stores. You can browse their entire collections and often find sales or discounts that you might not get in a physical store.
- PDF Patterns - Many online patterns come in a PDF format that you can print at home. While these require a bit of assembly (you'll need to tape the pages together), they're super convenient and often cheaper than printed patterns.

Free Patterns

Who doesn't love free stuff? Free patterns are a fantastic way to experiment with new techniques or styles without spending any money. Here are a few places to find them:

- Sewing Blogs - Many sewing bloggers and influencers offer free patterns to their readers. Websites like Tilly and the Buttons, Mood Fabrics, and Peppermint Magazine often feature free patterns for simple and stylish projects.
- Pinterest - Pinterest is a goldmine for free patterns. Just search for "free sewing patterns" and you'll discover a wide variety of projects, from clothes to home décor.
- Fabric Brands - Some fabric brands, like Robert Kaufman or Art Gallery Fabrics, offer free patterns on their websites that are designed to showcase their fabrics. These are often high-quality patterns perfect for beginners.
- Online Sewing Communities - Joining online sewing communities like PatternReview.com or Reddit's r/sewing can lead you to even more free patterns shared by fellow sewing enthusiasts.

Libraries

Yes, your local library might be another resource! Some libraries have collections of sewing books that include patterns or offer digital access to pattern databases. Plus, you can often borrow sewing books that contain a variety of patterns, which is a great way to test out new designs without any cost.

CHAPTER 8

Types of Fabric

Fabric Guide

Types of Fabric, Choosing the Right One, and Working with Different Textiles

Fabric is the heart of every sewing project, and choosing the right one is key to achieving the look and feel you want. Each fabric type has its own qualities and characteristics, which can make or break your sewing project. In this chapter, we'll explore the different types of fabric, how to choose the right one for your project, and some helpful tips on working with various textiles.

Types of Fabric

Understanding the different fabric types is essential for selecting the perfect material for your sewing project. Fabrics can be classified into several categories based on their fibers and how they are woven or knitted.

1. Natural Fabrics
- Cotton: Soft, breathable, and easy to work with, cotton is the most popular fabric for beginners. It comes in many variations, such as quilting cotton, broadcloth, and muslin. It's great for making garments, home décor, and accessories. Use it for dresses, shirts, skirts, home décor, and quilting.
- Linen: Made from the flax plant, linen is known for its crisp texture and lightness. It wrinkles easily, but it's incredibly

breathable and cool, making it a great summer fabric. Use it for summer clothes like dresses, blouses, pants, and lightweight home goods.
- Wool: A warm, insulating fabric, wool is made from animal fleece. It's typically used for outerwear like coats, jackets, and winter garments. Use it for coats, suits, skirts, and jackets.
- Silk: A luxurious fabric, silk has a soft, shiny surface and a fluid drape. It's delicate and requires special care but makes beautiful garments. Use it for dresses, blouses, scarves, and evening wear.

2. Synthetic Fabrics
- Polyester: A versatile and durable fabric, polyester is resistant to shrinking and wrinkles. It's commonly blended with other fibers to enhance their durability. Use it for everyday wear, activewear, outerwear, and home décor.
- Nylon: Known for its strength and resistance to abrasion, nylon is often used for activewear and outerwear. Use it for sportswear, jackets, raincoats, and bags.
- Rayon: Made from plant fibers, rayon is lightweight and has a beautiful drape. It can be tricky to sew with, as it can shrink and stretch out of shape. Use it for dresses, skirts, blouses, and linings.
- Spandex/Lycra: These stretchy fabrics are known for their ability to return to their original shape. They're typically

blended with other fabrics to give them a bit of stretch. Use it for activewear, swimsuits, leggings, and fitted garments.

3. Blended Fabrics
- Cotton/Polyester Blend: A combination of the softness of cotton with the durability and wrinkle resistance of polyester. It's easy to care for and holds up well over time. Use it for everyday clothing, sheets, and light home décor.
- Wool/Polyester Blend: Offers the warmth and luxury of wool with the durability and wrinkle resistance of polyester. Use it for coats, suits, and jackets.

Tips for Choosing the Right Fabric

Selecting the right fabric can be daunting, especially for beginners. Here are some tips to help you choose the perfect fabric for your project:

1. Consider the Project Type: Think about the garment or item you're making. Is it something that needs to hold its shape (like a structured jacket) or something that needs to flow (like a dress)? Fabrics like cotton, linen, and wool can hold structure, while silk and rayon offer a flowing, draped effect.

2. Think About the Season: For summer garments, lightweight fabrics like cotton, linen, and rayon are perfect because they are breathable and cool. For winter garments, heavier fabrics like wool and polyester blends are ideal for warmth and insulation.

3. **Know the Fabric's Drape:** The drape of a fabric refers to how it falls when hung. Fabrics with a soft drape, like silk and rayon, create flowing, graceful garments, while stiffer fabrics like cotton and linen hold their shape better. Consider the drape when choosing fabric for your project.

4. **Match the Fabric to Your Skill Level:** As a beginner, it's best to start with easy-to-handle fabrics like cotton, which are forgiving and simple to sew. Avoid delicate or tricky fabrics like silk or velvet until you gain more experience with your machine.

5. **Check the Fabric Weight:** Fabric weight refers to the thickness of the material. Lighter-weight fabrics are ideal for blouses, dresses, and summer garments, while heavier-weight fabrics are better for jackets, coats, and upholstery. Be sure to choose a weight that suits the design of your project.

6. **Consider the Fabric Care:** Different fabrics require different care. Some fabrics like wool and silk, need dry cleaning or hand washing, while others like cotton and polyester blends, can be machine-washed. Make sure to check the care instructions before purchasing fabric.

How to Work with Different Textiles

Once you've chosen your fabric, it's important to know how to work with it to achieve the best results. Here are some tips for working with common textiles:

1. Cotton
- Cotton is easy to sew and press. Make sure to pre-wash it to prevent shrinking. Use a universal needle and medium tension settings when sewing with cotton.
- Pro Tip: Use a walking foot when sewing many layers of cotton, especially for quilting.

2. Linen
- Linen wrinkles easily, so it's important to press the fabric regularly as you sew. You can also add a little starch to help it maintain its shape.
- Pro Tip: Use a sharp needle to avoid snags, and always press with steam to get crisp seams.

3. Wool
- Wool fabrics should be sewn with a ballpoint needle to avoid damaging the fibers. When pressing wool, use a pressing cloth to avoid direct contact with the iron and prevent shine.
- Pro Tip: Pre-shrink wool fabric by washing it before cutting.

4. Silk

- Silk is delicate and can be slippery to work with. Use a fine needle (size 9 or 11) and avoid pins, as they can leave marks on the fabric. Instead, use fabric weights or a basting stitch to hold the pieces together.
- Pro Tip: Work with silk in a well-lit space, and keep the fabric taut while sewing to avoid puckering.

5. Polyester

- Polyester is easy to sew and doesn't wrinkle easily. It's also a durable fabric, making it perfect for everyday wear.
- Pro Tip: Use a universal or stretch needle depending on the amount of stretch the fabric has.

6. Nylon

- Nylon fabrics can be a bit tricky, as they can melt if exposed to high heat. Always use a low-heat iron and avoid pressing directly on the fabric. Sew with a polyester thread, as it blends well with nylon.
- Pro Tip: When working with nylon, be careful with pins as they can leave permanent holes in the fabric.

7. Rayon

- Rayon can be slippery and stretchy, making it a bit challenging to work with. Always pre-wash rayon before sewing, as it tends to shrink. Use a ballpoint needle for smooth stitching.

- Pro Tip: Sew rayon with a walking foot to prevent it from slipping or shifting.

Choosing the right fabric is an important step in ensuring your project turns out just the way you envision it. By understanding the types of fabric, knowing how to choose the right one for your project, and following some simple tips for working with various textiles, you'll feel more confident in your sewing skills.

CHAPTER 9

Finishing Seams

**How to Finish Seams
without a Serger**

Creating Clean, Professional Edges

One of the key aspects of sewing that makes your projects look polished and professional is how you finish the seams. A raw seam left untrimmed or unfinished can fray and unravel, causing your garment to lose shape or weaken over time. In this chapter, we'll explore several techniques for finishing seams, from simple to more advanced methods, so you can achieve a neat, durable finish every time.

Why Finish Seams?

Seam finishing serves a few purposes:
- Prevents Fraying: Most fabrics (especially natural fibers like cotton and linen) have a tendency to fray at the edges when washed or worn. Finishing the seams keeps your fabric from unravelling.
- Strengthens the Seam: Properly finished seams are less likely to split or tear when under tension or stress.
- Improves the Look: Neat, clean edges help elevate the overall quality and professionalism of your garment or project.
- Adds Durability: Finished seams make your project last longer, ensuring it holds up to wear and tear.

Common Seam Finishing Techniques

There are many ways to finish seams, each with its advantages and ideal uses. Let's go over the most common methods and when to use them.

Vintage and Thrift Stores

If you love a retro vibe, don't overlook vintage stores, thrift shops, and even estate sales. These places can be goldmines for finding unique, out-of-print patterns that you won't find anywhere else. Just be sure to check that the pattern pieces are intact and the instructions are included before buying.

1. **Overcasting or Zigzag Stitching**
   - How It Works: Overcasting (or zigzag stitching) uses a zigzag stitch to encase the raw edge of the fabric. This method helps prevent fraying and gives the seam a clean finish.
   - Best For: Light to medium-weight fabrics like cotton, polyester, and lightweight linen.
   - How to Do It:
     - Set your sewing machine to a zigzag stitch with a narrow width.
     - Place the raw edge of your fabric under the foot, making sure the needle swings slightly over the edge with each stitch.
     - Sew along the entire raw edge, keeping the fabric taut but not stretched.
   - Tip: Use a walking foot if you're working with thicker fabrics or multiple layers to ensure an even stitch.

2. **French Seams**
   - How It Works: French seams are a more refined way of finishing seams, creating an enclosed finish that hides the raw edges completely. This technique is ideal for delicate fabrics like silk, chiffon, or lightweight cotton.
   - Best For: Sheer or delicate fabrics that you want to have a clean, professional finish.
   - How to Do It:

- First, sew the seam with the fabric right sides together using a ¼-inch seam allowance.
- Trim the seam allowance slightly and press it to one side.
- Next, press the seam open, then fold the fabric so that the wrong sides are together, enclosing the raw edges inside the folded seam.
- Sew again along the seam, using a slightly larger seam allowance (usually around 3/8 inch).
- Press the seam to one side.
* Tip: This technique works especially well for garments like blouses, dresses, or lightweight skirts that need a clean and polished interior.

3. Bias Tape or Bias Binding

* How It Works: Bias tape is a narrow strip of fabric cut on the bias (diagonal to the grain of the fabric) and sewn around the raw edges of the seam. This method is great for adding color or a decorative touch, as well as preventing fraying.
* Best For: Projects where you want to add a decorative touch, such as with quilts, hems, or neckline finishes.
* How to Do It:
  - Cut strips of bias tape that are slightly longer than the raw edges of your fabric.
  - Open the bias tape and pin it along the edge of your seam.

- Sew the bias tape along the raw edge of the fabric, then fold the bias tape over the edge and stitch it down, encasing the raw edge.
- Tip: Make sure to press the bias tape flat before sewing to ensure it lays nicely.

4. Serger or Overlock Stitching
- How It Works: A serger or overlock machine trims the fabric edges and stitches them all in one step. The overlock stitch prevents fraying by enclosing the fabric edges in thread. This is the most professional and durable way to finish seams.
- Best For: Heavy fabrics or any project that will be washed frequently, such as activewear, children's clothes, or home décor.
- How to Do It:
  - Place the fabric under the serger foot and sew along the raw edge. The machine will trim the edge while simultaneously stitching it in place.
- Tip: If you don't have a serger, some sewing machines have built-in overlock stitches that mimic the effect.

6. Pinked Seams
- How It Works: Pinking shears are scissors with a serrated edge that trim fabric while creating a zigzag finish. This method helps prevent fraying by cutting the fabric at an angle.

- Best For: Light fabrics that don't fray easily, like polyester or cotton blends.
- How to Do It:
  - After sewing your seam, use pinking shears to trim along the raw edge of the fabric.
- Tip: Pinked seams don't provide as much protection from fraying as other methods, so they work best on fabrics that don't unravel easily.

7. Lapped Seams

- How It Works: Lapped seams are often used in denim, outerwear, and heavy fabrics. The seam is sewn with one edge of the fabric overlapping the other. This method is great for adding strength to seams that will endure heavy wear.
- Best For: Denim, heavy wool, and outerwear garments.
- How to Do It:
  - Place the fabric pieces together with the raw edges slightly overlapping.
  - Sew along the edge, making sure the fabric is securely in place.
- Tip: Lapped seams are often topstitched to add an extra layer of strength and give the garment a professional look.

Mastering the art of seam finishing is an essential skill that elevates your sewing projects. Practice these techniques, and soon you'll be finishing seams like a pro!

CHAPTER 10

First Project Recommendations

For the impatient beginner, I recommend starting with projects that matter to YOU. If pillows in random patterns don't appeal to you, then try something wearable because you can be proud of it and it offers the opportunity to show it off. The point is to make something, ANYTHING to get the practice you need to be great.

Pillow Case

A pillow or pillow case project offers the opportunity for a quick win. You can practice your cutting and measuring skills, practice sewing straight, and learn to hem. Here's the steps.

Pick a fabric - something that is soft and comfortable against the skin. Cotton is a popular choice for pillowcases. Satin is great for the hair and skin as well.

Cut your pieces - For a standard pillowcase, cut two pieces of fabric measuring 21 inches wide by 31 inches long. This includes a 1/2-inch seam allowance on all sides and a 4-inch hem allowance for the opening. For a king pillowcase, cut two pieces of fabric measuring 21 inches wide by 41 inches long. Lay the pieces so that good sides are touching.

Sew - Pin or clip along both long sides and one of the short sides. Leave the other short side (the opening) unpinned. Sew along the pinned edges with a 1/2-inch seam allowance, backstitching at the beginning and end to secure the stitches. Finish the raw edges with a zigzag stitch or pinking shears to prevent fraying.

Hem - On the unsewn short edge (the opening), fold the edge over 1/2 inch towards the wrong side of the fabric and press with an iron. Fold over again by 4 inches and press to create a neat hem. Sew close to the inner folded edge of the hem, ensuring you catch both layers of fabric. Backstitch at the beginning and end for extra security.

Finish - Turn the pillowcase right side out and push out the corners with a point turner or the end of a pencil. Press the pillowcase with an iron to create crisp edges. Check all seams to ensure they are secure and free of gaps. Trim any loose threads. Slide your pillow into the newly sewn pillowcase. Smooth out any wrinkles, and you're done!

Skirt with Elastic Band

An elastic waist skirt is just about the easiest garment to make since it's only a rectangle gathered by elastic in the waist. This project will help you learn how to utilize your measuring skills.

Pick a fabric - You can pick any kind of fabric for this project, but since we're just starting out let's go for a cotton or mid weight knit.

Do the Math - For a quick flared skirt, cut a piece of fabric that is 1.5X your hip measurement by your desired length plus 4 inches. 3 inches will be for the waistband and 1 inch for the bottom hem. Here's an example below.

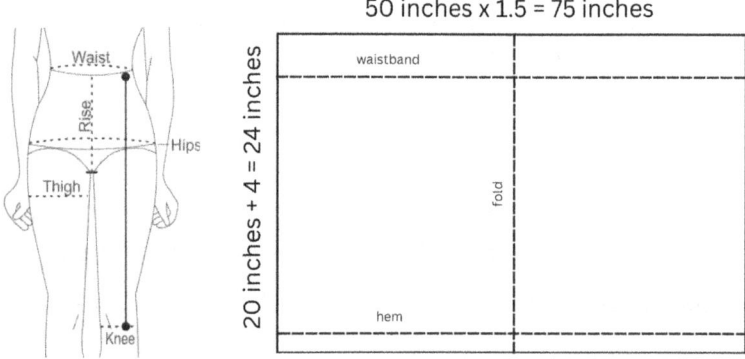

HIPS: 50 inches

KNEE: 20 inches

Sew - Fold the fabric in half with the right sides facing each other and sew down the length of the skirt with a 1/2-inch seam allowance, backstitching at the beginning and end to secure the stitches. Finish the raw edges with a zigzag stitch or pinking shears to prevent fraying.

Hem - Fold both the top and bottom edge over 1/2 inch towards the wrong side of the fabric and press with an iron. Fold over the top edge again by 2-1/2 inches and press to create a neat hem. Fold over the bottom edge again by 1/2 inch and press. Sew both hems close to the inner folded edge of the hem, ensuring you catch both layers of fabric. Leave a 1 inch opening in the waistband seam.

Elastic - Wrap a piece of 1" elastic around your waist and stretch until it fits snug the way you want the skirt to fit. Cut the end with a 1 inch overlap. Secure a safety pin through the end of the elastic and push it though the seam opening left in the waist band all the way around until it comes out on the other side. Overlap the ends of the elastic by 1 inch and sew them together. Push the elastic completely in the waistband and sew the opening closed.

Finish - Turn the skirt right side out and check all seams to ensure they are secure and free of gaps. Trim any loose threads, and you're done!

Ruffle Tote Bag

This is my favorite project for impatient beginners because although it's not the easiest, it will teach you all the basic skills to conquer so many more projects.

Pick a fabric - Any woven non-stretchy fabric will work great for this project.

Cut your pieces - Start by ironing your fabric to remove wrinkles and make it easier to work with. Fold the fabric in half, lining it up to ensure you have two layers. Cut two 10-1/2 inch by 13 inch rectangles for the tote bag. For the ruffles, cut two strips of fabric that are 4 inches wide and 26 inches long. For the straps, cut two more strips tha 3 inches wide by 26 inches long.

Sew the straps - Fold the strap fabric in half with the good sides touching, and pin along the long edge. Sew along the edge of each strap, starting with a backstitch to secure the seam. Use a pencil or paintbrush to help turn the strap right side out. Iron the straps flat, ensuring the seam is on the side.

Create the Ruffle - Fold the ruffle strips in half along the long side with the good sides touching, and sew the short sides closed. Turn the ruffle right side out and iron it flat.

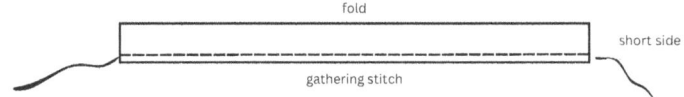

Sewing a Gathering Stitch - To gather the ruffle, increase your sewing machine's tension and stitch length to the maximum, then sew along the long edge. Leave long threads at both ends. Pull the bobbin thread gently to create gathers along the fabric.

Attach the Straps - Fold down the top edge of your tote bag fabric by 1/4" inch and iron flat. Then fold it again by 3/4 inch. Iron it to set the fold. Place the ends of the straps inside the folded edge and pin them in place. Ensure the straps are even and secure. Sew along the edge of the folded fabric close to the inner folded edge of the hem to attach the straps, adjusting your machine settings back to a regular stitch length and tension.

Attach the Ruffle - Line up the edge of the ruffle with one long edge of the tote bag on the good side of the fabric aligning the top of the ruffle with the top of the bag. Pin the ruffle in place, ensuring it's even and flat. Line up the other ruffle to the opposite edge of the tote bag. Sew the ruffle to the fabric, then place the second tote bag rectangle on top, with the good sides facing inwards. Pin and sew the sides and bottom edges of the bag together, using a 1/2 inch seam allowance. Use a backstitch at the beginning and end to secure the seams.

Finish the Bag - Turn the bag right side out to check the seams and ensure everything looks good. To finish the seams and prevent fraying, trim any excess fabric on the inside and turn the bag right side out. You can create a French seam by sewing a topstitch along the edges. Iron the bag flat to give it a polished look. Enjoy your new ruffle tote bag!

CHAPTER 11

Final Words of Encouragement

Congratulations! You've conquered the basics and have started your sewing journey- that's no small feat. Remember when you first started, how those fabric pieces seemed like a jigsaw puzzle, and the sewing machine felt like it was speaking a foreign language? Well, look at you now! You've tackled stitches, seams, and patterns with confidence, and you've got tangible, beautiful projects to show for it, *or at least you're getting there.*

Sewing is like anything else in life—it's about progress, not perfection. Every time you thread that needle or cut into a new piece of fabric, you're creating something unique that didn't exist before. That's powerful. So when you make a mistake, embrace it. It's just a part of the journey that will make you a stronger, more resilient creator.

Your sewing journey doesn't end here; it's just beginning. And let me tell you, there are so many exciting paths to explore!

Next Steps to Take

Practice - Sew something... ANYTHING. Any time you take that sewing machine out and make at least one stitch, it counts. Alternations count. Fixing hems count. Continue practicing the basics, but don't be afraid to challenge yourself with new techniques. The more you sew, the more natural it will feel.

Start a Sewing Journal - Document your projects, ideas, and even mistakes. It's a great way to track your growth and keep your creativity flowing.

Join a Sewing Community or Class - Whether online or in-person, being part of a sewing community can provide support, inspiration, and new ideas. You'll find that there's always something new to learn from others. And if you're ever in the Houston, TX area, check out our amazing sewing classes and events at BlueprintDIY.com/sewing-classes.

Experiment with Different Fabrics - Don't limit yourself to just cotton or denim. Experiment with silk, knit, or even leather to expand your skills.

Take on Bigger Projects - Once you're comfortable with the basics, try tackling more complex projects like garments, quilts, or home decor. These projects will push you to refine your techniques and think creatively.

Keep Learning - There are countless resources available—from books and blogs to YouTube channels like BlueprintDIY and classes. Keep feeding your curiosity and sharpening your skills.

Remember, every stitch you make is a step forward. Your sewing journey is unique, just like the pieces you create. So keep going, stay curious, and never stop learning. You've got this!

Glossary

Back Stitch - A back stitch is a reverse stitch used to secure the beginning and end of a seam. By stitching forward a few stitches, then reversing over those stitches, and finally stitching forward again, the back stitch prevents seams from unraveling and adds durability to your project.

Basting- Temporary, loose stitches to gather fabric or hold something in place. You can do it by hand or by using the longest stitch length on your sewing machine. When you are machine basting, loosen the top tension for easier removal.

Bias Binding- Strips of fabric cut on a 45-degree angle to the selvage. In this direction, the fabric is stretchy, and it adjusts well to curves, making it a great finish for necklines, (curved) hems or armholes. The strip is used to encase the raw edge of a hem or a seam. By using a contrasting or a piece of patterned fabric you can add a pop of color to the inside of a garment.

Buttonhole- A reinforced hole in the fabric slightly bigger than the button that needs to pass through it. Most sewing machines have a buttonhole foot and can make a beautiful buttonhole in 4 steps. Or you can make them using a zig-zag stitch on a sewing machine, or by hand using a blanket stitch. Whatever the project is, always make a few test buttonholes to see if you need heavier fusible interfacing to get a good result. Making a test buttonhole is also a good way to see how the color thread you chose looks with your main fabric and to check if your button easily passes through the hole. You need to make the buttonholes and open them up first before you place the buttons. Line up the edges of the two button stands and poke a marking pen through the buttonholes to mark the button placement. It's easy and you will always have the buttons line up perfectly with the buttonholes.

Casing – a fabric tunnel or channel that is created to hold and guide something such as elastic, a drawstring, or a cord. It's commonly used in waistbands, cuffs, hems, and drawstring bags to provide a finished way to insert and secure elastic or ties.

Cut on fold- When a pattern says to cut a pattern piece on fold, it means you need to align that edge to the fabric fold. That way you only have to cut out half of the pattern piece (don't cut the fold), but when you unfold the fabric, you have a full symmetrical piece of your garment. This is often the case for a bodice front without a center seam or a bodice back without a center back seam.

Darts- Darts are used to shape the garment around the waist, bust, shoulders, and sometimes sleeves. They are often shaped like triangles or diamonds.

Double-fold hem- A hem that's folded towards the inside of the garment, the raw edge folded first toward the wrong side of the fabric, and then a second fold again towards the inside of the garment encasing the raw edge.

Facing - Facing is a way to finish the raw fabric edges, stabilize, add structure, and strength. They are a partial lining often made from the main fabric and are used on necklines and armholes. Facing can be a separate panel or cut-on facing. Cut on facings are part of the panel they are facing. Cut on facings are often used in a waterfall neckline or a button band. Facings are often used in combination with interfacing.

French Seams- French seams are a great way to finish your fabric if you don't have a serger because the French seam encases the raw edge of your fabric. This technique is mostly used on straight seams, but with a bit of practice, the technique works well on curved seams. If you venture into curved seams, I suggest you keep the seam allowance narrow, because wider seams will pucker easily. Snipping your seam allowance around the curve will also help prevent puckering. In general, you can use a narrow seam allowance for lightweight fabrics and a wider seam allowance as the weight of your fabric increases.

Gather- Gathered fabric is used to create fullness or ruffles. Sew one or two lines of gathering stitches just inside and/or outside the stitch line. Use a long stitch length (5mm and up) on your sewing machine and loosen the top tension on your sewing machine for easier gathering. Don't back tack when you start stitching and leave long thread tails. Anchor the thread tails on one side around a pin, and carefully hold the loose (top or bottom) thread tails and slide the fabric you want to gather along the thread.

Godet: A triangular piece of fabric inserted into a skirt to widen the bottom to add movement and fullness. Is also used in sleeves and bell-bottomed pants.

Gusset: In a garment, a gusset is a triangular piece of fabric inserted into a seam to add roominess. In bags, a gusset is used to pinch in the corners to create a bottom from the sides.

Hem- The bottom edge of a garment often folded up towards the inside of the garment.

Interfacing- An additional layer of fabric that is used to stabilize, add structure, "crispness" and strength. It lays between the lining/facing and the outer fabric of a garment.

Invisible zipper- This zipper is sewn with a special presser foot and seams. when it's done right it's hard to see the zipper in the seam, hence the name.

Lining - A layer of fabric on the inside of a garment to hide construction seams and details, add warmth and make it more comfortable to wear and easier to put on.

Nap - Some fabrics, like velvet or velour have a pile, and the fibers don't quite lay vertically, but in a particular direction. This is known as the nap. You can feel the nap if you run your hand back and forth across the fabric. The nap should run downwards in the project.

Needle Auto Up/Down Button - The auto up/down button is a feature found on some sewing machines that allows you to control the position of the needle when you stop sewing. Pressing this button will raise or lower the needle automatically, making it easier to pivot fabric, start new seams, or finish a stitch without losing your place.

Notions - Small accessories used to aid in sewing: scissors, needles, thread, seam ripper, zippers, etc.

One-Step Buttonhole - A one-step buttonhole is a sewing machine feature that allows you to create a complete buttonhole in just one step. With this feature, the machine automatically stitches all four sides of the buttonhole without needing to manually adjust the fabric or settings, making it quick and easy to add buttonholes to your project.

Pattern – A template on paper or cardboard from which all of the pieces of the garment are traced onto fabric. All the parts are then cut out and assembled to create the final piece.

Placket - an opening in a garment that allows it to be put on or taken off more easily, typically reinforced with extra fabric or stitching and often finished with buttons, snaps, or a zipper. Plackets are commonly found in shirts, blouses, dresses, and sleeves.

Pleat – A type of fold in the fabric created by doubling the material back on itself and securing it in place. When ironed, they create a sharp crease.

Right side / Wrong side - The right side of the fabric is the side you want to see on the outside of the garment. The wrong side is the backside of a fabric and the inside of the garment. Sometimes they look the same; in that case, pick a side and stick with it.

Seam- The line where you sew together two pieces of fabric. There are different seams like a straight or flat felled seam.

Seam allowance- The fabric between the edge of the fabric and the stitch line. The width can vary between pattern companies and in a garment. Always check the pattern descriptions and pattern pieces.

Some commonly used seam allowances are:
- 0.6 cm / 1/4"
- 1 cm / 3/8"
- 1.6 cm / 5/8"
- 2.5 cm / 1"

Narrow seam allowances are great used on curves and for special seam finishes, like a French seam. Wider seam allowances can also be used for certain special finishes like French seams on heavier fabrics, flat-felled seams, or when you might want to adjust the fit.

Stitch in the ditch- Stitch in the seam line, pulling it slightly open on both sides. By stitching in from the outside of the garment, through all the layers, you can invisibly secure a facing or a turned-up sleeve cuff. You can also stitch-in-the-ditch when you are attaching bias binding.

Straight stitch -The most basic machine stitch, that produces a single row of straight, even stitches. It's used to construct a garment and for topstitching.

Selvage- The edge of a woven fabric produced during the manufacturing process. This edge keeps the fabric from raveling.

Speed Control - Speed control is a feature on some sewing machines that allows you to adjust the sewing speed. Whether you're working on a delicate fabric and need to slow down, or you're piecing together long seams and want to speed up, the speed control slider or dial gives you the flexibility to sew at a pace that suits you.

Tension - The amount of "pinching" done to your thread as it flows through your sewing machine. Thicker fabrics need a higher tension (a harder pinch so the thread doesn't flow out too quickly), and thinner fabrics need less tension (a lesser pinch to let the thread out easily to prevent puckering).

Top Stitch - A top stitch is a row of stitching on the outside of a garment, usually done close to the edge or seam, that serves both functional and decorative purposes. It adds strength to the seam and helps the fabric lay flat while giving your project a polished, professional look. Top stitching is often used on hems, collars, and along seams.

Walking Foot- A presser foot that helps feed multiple layers of fabric through your sewing machine more evenly. A walking foot is often used by quilters because it helps to evenly transport the layers trough the sewing machine.

Notes

The Impatient Beginner's Guide to Sewing

Notes

The Impatient Beginner's Guide to Sewing

Sewing Practice 1 - Practice guiding the paper to sew in a straight line. Set sewing machine tension slightly looser. Try between 4 and 5.

Sewing Practice 2 - Practice turning corners. Start at one end and sew to the corner. Stop at the corner and put your needle down and your presser foot up. Turn the paper so that the line is in front of you. Put your presser foot back down and start sewing again to the next corner. Repeat until you get to the end.

Sewing Practice 3 - Practice curvy lines. Start at one end and guide the paper to stay on the line. Go slow and use a shorter stitch length like 2.5 for more control.

Sewing Practice 4 - Practice changing directions. Start at one point and sew to a turning point. Use the same technique as Sewing Practice 2.

Sewing Practice 5 - Practice sewing in a circle. Start sewing at any point on the circle and use your hands to guide the paper along the line as you sew.

Sewing Practice 6 - Practice sewing shapes. Go slow and turn corners using the needle down technique. Putting the needle down to turn helps to keep your place while adjusting fabric so that your seam will be nice and consistent at the end.

Tear away sheets to practice sewing.

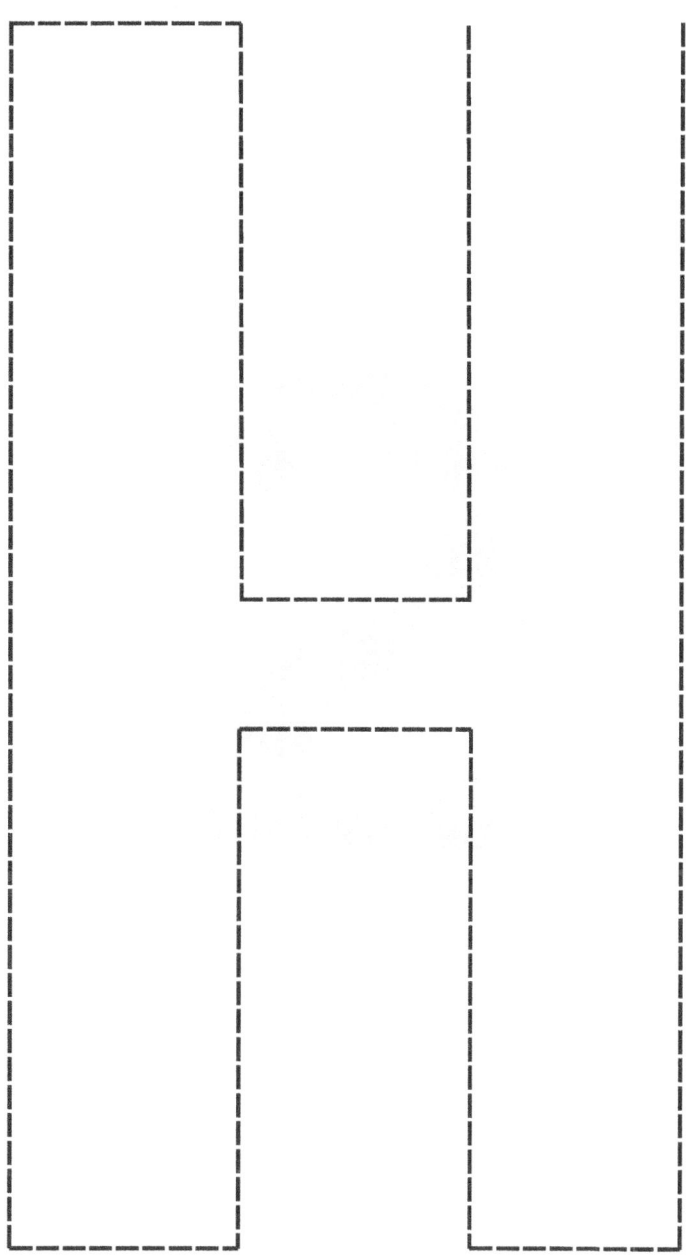

The Impatient Beginner's Guide to Sewing

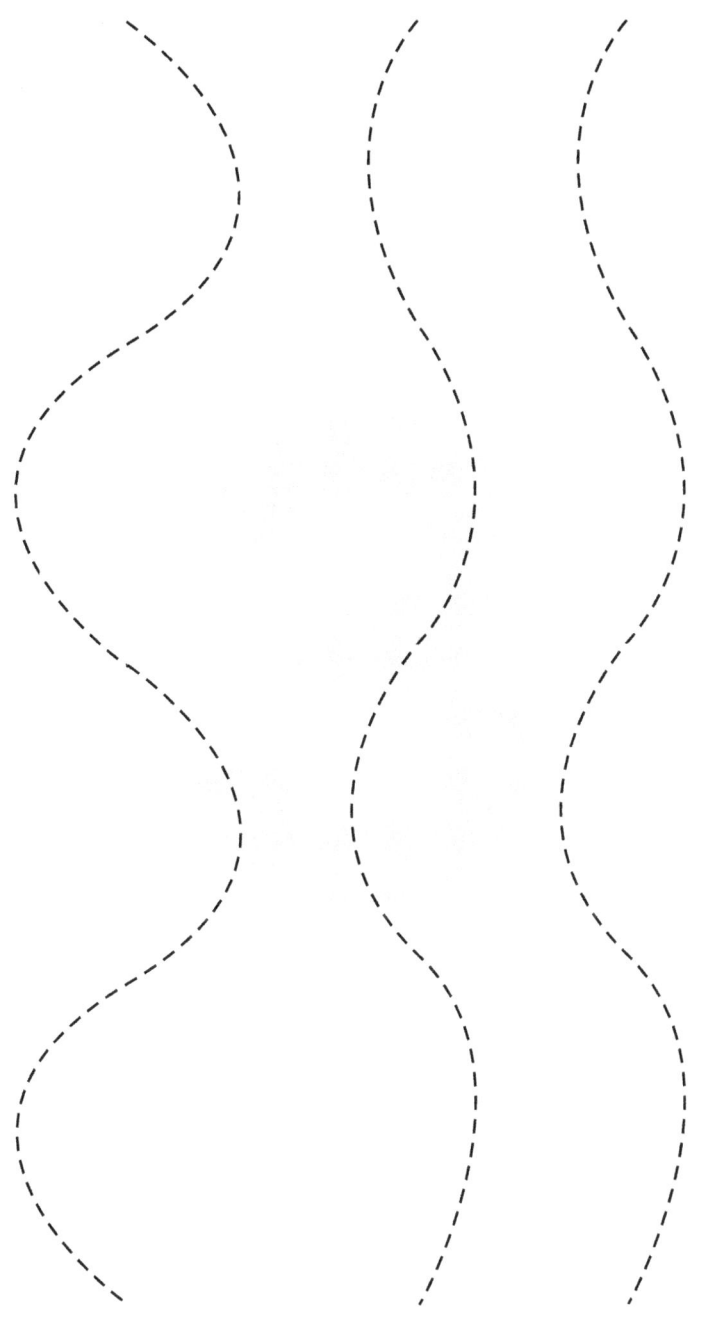

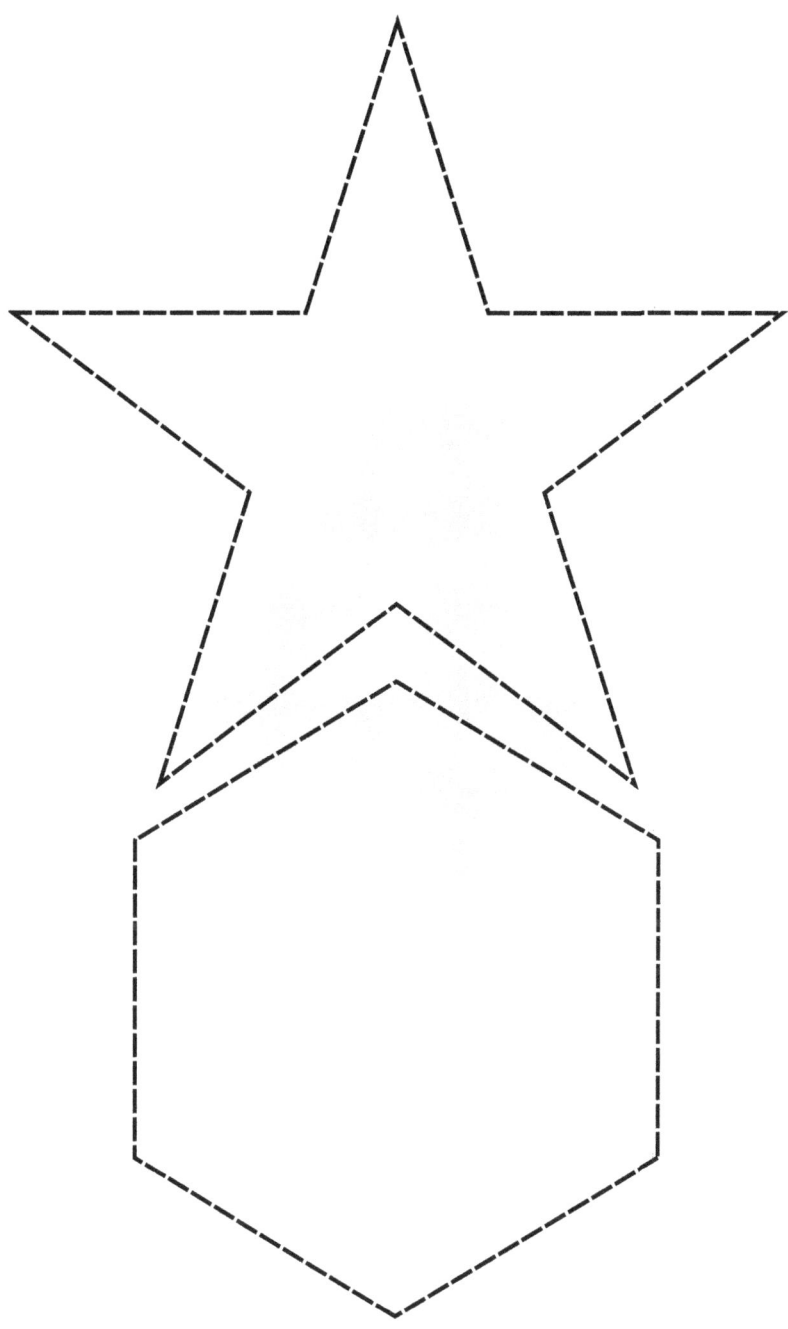

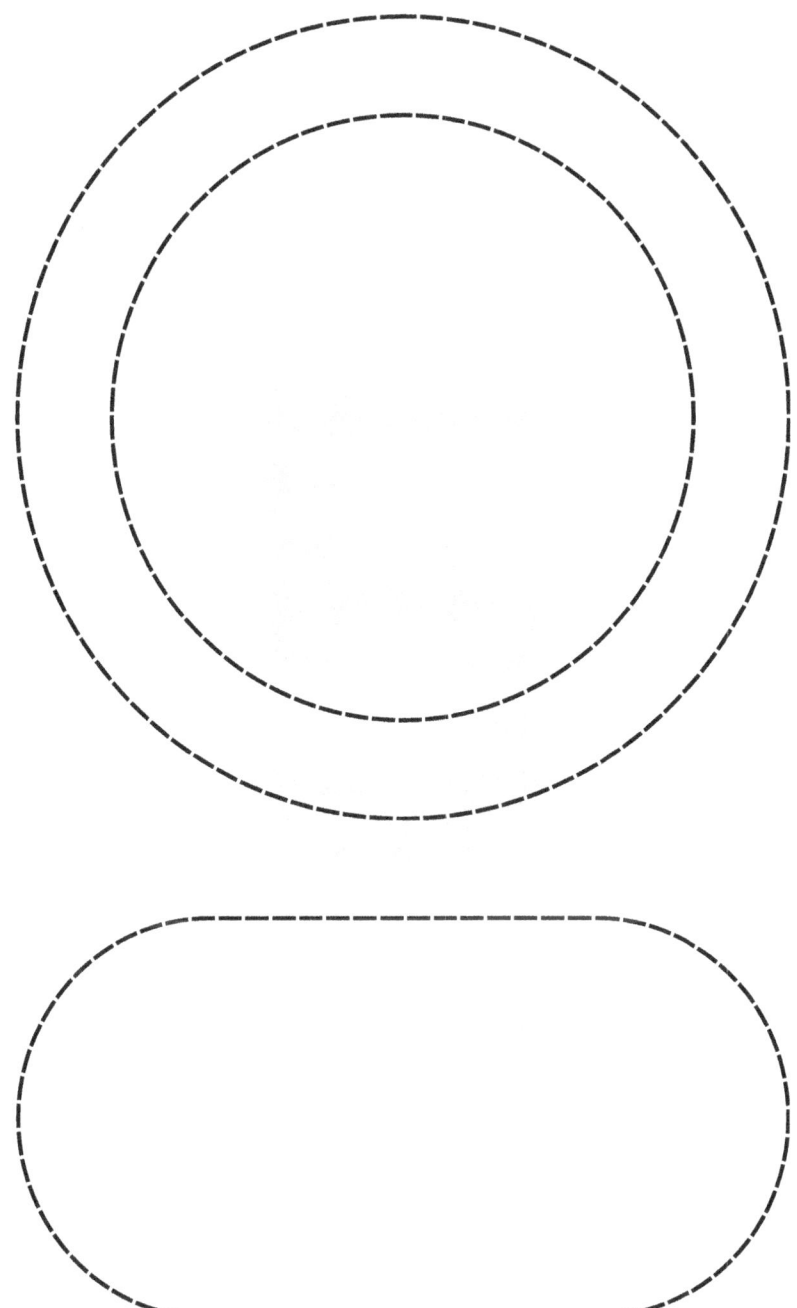

Download and Print more practice pages here.

Made in the USA
Coppell, TX
21 February 2026

71974989R10066